Living Li[

In the 4th Quarter

Leaving a Godly Legacy

Donald Zoller

Foreword — Charlotte Adelsperger

Living Life in the 4th Quarter – Leaving a Godly Legacy

Copyright © 2016 by Donald Zoller

Table of Contents

A Word of Thanks

I find writing a book takes more than just the author. Although it does not take a village, a creative graphic artist and a few critical readers are a plus—people who are honest and forthright with their edits and comments. In this regard, it isn't too difficult to say "thank you" to those who, out of a labor of love, contributed so much in making this book a positive reading experience and practical guide. My intention is to give appropriate and deserved credit to those involved, but I wonder about the people I may have forgotten—some who have been waiting years for this book.

First, I want to give special thanks to *Mike Bayly*, a faithful leader of a men's Bible study in Kansas City. For several years, he kept reminded me to write this book. A true friend!

I also want to say "thank you" to *Joe Lenard*, a friend for so many years and my co-author of *The Last Shofar! – What the Fall Feasts of the Lord are Telling the Church* (2014). Joe and *Bob Brown,* Joe's friend, did a masterful job of raking through the text at least three different times for spelling, punctuation and other grammatical stuff, as well as content consistency. A big job, and much appreciated!

Rod Laughlin, a friend and critical reader, freely tells me things I need to hear to make the book a better read. He was a great help in reviewing the text. *Don Reed*, an editor of doctorial thesis publications, added his professional review of the book. Ever looking for opportunities for marketing the book, *Charlotte Adelsperger* freely gave of her time both as a critical reader, and by presenting strategies for how best to get the book into the reader's hand. She also kindly and enthusiastically wrote the Foreword for this book. A heartfelt thanks to you all.

Most of all, I thank the Lord by allowing me the privilege of serving His people by writing about *Living Life in the 4th Quarter*. May He help each of us leave a godly legacy.

Foreword

Charlotte Adelsperger
Author and Speaker

When Don Zoller speaks to a group or teaches a Bible study, he brings a flow of rich insights and lots of enthusiasm. People don't want to miss any of it! He's scriptural, prayerful and well prepared. Most of all, Don impacts lives in a lasting way.

Likewise there's impact through Don's latest work, *Living Life in the 4th Quarter.* He offers a timely and helpful read for any of us in the latter part of our lives. More than anything Don wants to witness to the wonder and greatness of God. He challenges us to play well, to keep an intimate relationship with God through Christ. He encourages us to express our love to family and to take time to share about God's faithfulness. He calls it, "Paying a lot of attention to the really important stuff."

But will our children, grandchildren and others remember the "important stuff?" Don's approach is akin to what author Henry Blackaby says in *Experiencing God:* "Talk with your children about God's activity."

Both authors urge us to recount how we met Christ personally and how He called us into His mission on this earth. We are to share divine surprises as well as "ups and downs." The Psalmist gives a clear focus: "So teach us to number our days that we may get a heart of wisdom." (Psalm 90:12)

It's always special to tell how I know author Don Zoller. My husband Bob and I met Don and his wife Bev in 2008 when they moved to the Kansas City area. They joined our church, and became a warm and vital part of a study group that met in our home. Soon we discovered Don's gift of teaching. He presented outstanding material he had researched and written.

A few years later we learned Don's beloved Bev was suffering from dementia. In 2014 this dear couple moved to the Dallas, Texas area to be close to grandchildren. As Bev's illness got worse, Don began to write about the journey. Personal experiences turned into a remarkable book that has sustained many people: *This Ugly Disease – A Caregiver's Journey into Pain, Anguish and Hope.*

With that background, let's step into *Living Life in the 4th Quarter.* It covers a lot of beneficial things to do as one gets older. I found it to be a meaningful springboard to action! First, after reading Don's chapter about a cemetery, I felt prompted to stroll through a cemetery near our home. It was a beautiful September afternoon and I sensed God's presence.

For a long time I pondered memories of His faithfulness through the years. Thanksgiving and praise sang in my heart! I wondered how I might tell more of my story to family.

Then I came to an engraved headstone that grabbed my attention. It showed names of a married couple, George and Margaret. It read, "God's Work Was Truly Their Own." *This is an expression of the legacy Don Zoller talks about!* I thought. *Now what is God guiding **me** to do?*

When I got home, I opened my Bible and turned to the Apostle Paul's letter to the Ephesians. I've told my loved ones that I often pray Ephesians 3:14–19 for them and for myself. For me it's a "prayer letter" that closes with these words:

"... to know the love of Christ that surpasses knowledge, that you may be filled with all the fullness of God." (Ephesians 3:19)

I'm excited for every reader of *Life in the Fourth Quarter – Leaving a Godly Legacy!* It can be an amazing kick-off to an adventure with God's blessings all over it—for you and for those you love.

About This Book

Before I sit down to write a book, I always ask two questions: *Why* am I doing this? and *How* will the reader benefit from what I write? For the first question, there are really two reasons.

Mike Bayly is the first reason for writing this book. Mike is a good friend. He is also a leader of a Wednesday morning men's Bible study class in Kansas City. After I gave a study on *Living Life in the 4th Quarter* to the class, he was convinced that I should write a book from the material I presented. He has been waiting patiently for five years for this book to be written. "Where's the book?" was his frequent question. Without Mike's persistence, you probably would not be reading this book. I am thankful for his prodding and patience.

Why did it take so long to write such few pages? More than neglect, I believe it was in the Lord's timing to wait until now. Looking back, it is obvious that the complete story of *Living Life in the 4th Quarter* was not yet part of my life experience.

Here is the second reason why I wrote this book. Putting "pen to paper," I am now ready to talk about the things I am learning in the 4th quarter of my life. Yes, it is still a work in progress; but I think now I have a pretty good idea what the game is all about. In my 80th year, it is finally making some sense. Living in a community dedicated to senior living helps complete the picture. Over many cups of coffee, talking with those of similar age, I have gained much. I want to share these experiences with others so that they, too, can benefit and be encouraged.

This leads to the answer for my second question: *How can you, the reader, benefit from my 4th quarter life experience?* Hopefully, you will see yourself grappling with some of the same issues I discuss in the book. Together, we will discover that we are neither unique nor alone in this stage of life. I want us to be encouraged that there is a life to be lived with passion and purpose. I also want us to know that an intimate relationship with God really does matter, particularly in the 4th quarter.

A few months ago, I lost my wife, Beverley, to dementia at the age of 76. That loss spoke volumes to the brevity of life and how quickly it is spent. I am committed, more than ever, to leave behind a pile of stones—memorial stones that witness to the wonder and greatness of our God. My hope is that this book will be a stone in my pile. I want those stones to encourage and strengthen my children's faith, and the faith of their children, and the faith of the generations that follow. (Joshua 4:20–24)

What I wish for my family, I pray will also be the desire for your family and friends. May the fire of passion and commitment be lit so that God gets the glory from our lives as we live it in the 4th quarter.

Discussion questions follow each chapter. These are a thoughtful resource for personal study, with support groups, or for personal reflection. In either case, be sure to take notes as you read. Your notes will enrich your discussion time or personal reflections.

One final word. I am primarily writing to those who know Jesus Christ personally as a friend. Like the players in the game of football, they are the ones who will be the winners when they cross the goal line the final time at the end of the 4th quarter. This book is meant to stir their faith and keep them moving forward as they age.

Unquestionably, this book can be of benefit to those who do not share a similar Christian view of life. If by reading this book, you are encouraged to take the first step of faith toward Jesus Christ, so much the better. In any case, I believe the book will be a blessing as you join me on this journey into the 4th quarter of life.

Don Zoller, October 2016

A Beginning Word

What is your life? For you are a mist that appears for a little time and then vanishes. (James 4:14)

American football is a great game. The first game of American football was officially played on November 6, 1869 between two college teams, Rutgers and Princeton. By the rules of the game, it is played against the clock in four quarters of 15-minutes each. However, since the clock advances only when the ball is in play, the game typically takes two or more hours. Today, it is a great event for the entire family, for "tailgaters," or for those who just enjoy sitting around the flat-screen on a Sunday afternoon.

Just as the 4th quarter can be the most important quarter in the game of football, so can the final quarter be the most important of our life. Crossing the goal line the final time determines who wins the game, both in football and in life. But crossing the goal line does not come easy. The game is not played without a lot of rough-and-tumble and bruising experiences.

Join me as we look into just some of these hard and challenging experiences in the following chapters. If you are in the 4th quarter, you have survived the first three. Congratulations! But, it is the 4th quarter that is most demanding. It requires grit and every ounce of whatever strength you have left to complete the game, especially to complete it well. To be winners at the end of the game is the goal. It isn't for the fainthearted or for the benchwarmers. It's not a spectator sport. Like football, the last quarter is grueling and rigorous.

The opposing team will do whatever they can to keep you from winning. Personal stamina and determination will be challenged beyond limits. The issue is not *if* you are going to play in the 4th quarter, but rather *how well* are you going to play.

Just as in the game of football, our lives are played against the clock. However, we don't see a brightly lit scoreboard telling us when it is time to move from one quarter to the next. We just have this gut feeling that each new quarter brings change. Looking back over our shoulder, we can see how we have changed at various stages in our lives—education, career, marriage—or not—and for most, retirement. These events, and perhaps others, all describe change. Although the precise timing may be different for each of us, these phases often chart the journey we travel from one quarter of our lives to another. But, other forms of change also occur throughout the span of our lives.

We all experience change. We know these changes by what we are able to do, how we see our world, and by our reflection in the mirror. It was easier to do things *then* than it is *now*. Our behavior and temperament change, as does our view of life. With the passing of time, our political or social views may change—we engage the world around us differently. Looking at ourselves in the morning mirror tells the story of change. Of course, we can refuse to face reality, like the witch in the Snow White tale. It may be time for a new mirror! Even old photographs confirm the changes that happen over time.

Unlike in the game of football, we never have the option of running out the clock to our advantage. After all, we each have an appointed time when our life on earth will be over. Only the One who gives breath and life can take them away. Only God knows when the game will be over for us. We never know when we will get the call to come off the field, or if we will be given the opportunity for *overtime*. Unlike in the game of football, the clock is always in motion. *Whether the ball is in play or not, the quarters of life move forward. They are indeed very short!*

>And just as it is appointed for man to die once,
>and after that comes judgment . . . (Hebrews 9:27)

Therefore –

>. . . teach us to number our days that we may get a heart of wisdom. (Psalm 90:12)

No one can say for sure when life's quarters begin and end. It varies for each of us. But here is a general guide. The first quarter of life would be from infancy to about 25 years old, when formal education is behind us and the seeds of a career are beginning to sprout. The second quarter continues to about age 50, when most are comfortable with their career and family. The third quarter moves from 50 to when we start receiving Social Security and Medicare. Then 4th quarter starts, and it continues until the end of the game. Of course, there is always the potential for overtime—maybe a 100 plus. I know these are, at best, only approximations. Perhaps, they will help you place yourself in the quarter that is appropriate for you.

This is what I do know. Those in the first and second quarters of life look at older people as *old*. Those in the third quarter begin to sense that one day soon, they will be one of them. In the fourth quarter we realize that we have arrived. We are now one of those who we once thought were *old*.

The purpose of this book is to help you take a realistic look at the brevity of life. The game will soon be over. I want to encourage you. You are still on the green side of the grass if you are reading these words. It's not too late to live like the winner you are, or would like to be. It is not too late to leave a godly legacy, as this book later describes. From this book, I hope you will gain a clear vision for your future that will motivate you to live life to its fullest in your final quarter. This is the time of life to prepare for the next, not to conclude what you are now experiencing.

God has an eternal investment in each breath you take to reach the final goal, and He longs to say to you, *"Well done good and faithful servant."* If you are in the 4th quarter, *this book is for you!*

Chapter 1

A View from the Sidelines – A Walk Through the Cemetery

For everything there is a season, and a time for every matter under heaven: a time to be born, and a time to die ...
(Ecclesiastes 3:1–2)

Let's take a walk through the cemetery—of course, during the day. What we see are a lot of headstones. Some are upright; others are flat with the grass. These headstones indicate where the remains of people are buried. Coming closer, we notice that on each one is inscribed a very concise history of a person who used to be but is no more. Maybe there is a caption, "In Loving Memory," which is always nice to see. Of course, there is the name of the person and, perhaps, an indication of their relationship to the family. Then there are a couple of dates—when they were born and when they died, separated by *a dash*.

There will always be a dash between two dates, regardless how old or new the headstones might be. They could be located in an old historic section of the cemetery, where time has obscured most of the inscription; or they may be in one that is newer where the information can be plainly read. The words may be many, or may be few; they may be flamboyant with engraved carvings and even a photo—it doesn't matter. What they all share in common is the dash between two dates.

Have you ever stopped to think about the meaning of that little dash? Contained in that little mark, between the two dates, is the sum total of a person's life. Someday, your life will be represented by just a dash. Every breath you took, every thought you had or word you spoke, everything you did, and everything you were is summed up in that short little dash between the two dates. With each passing generation, as your life story fades, the meaning of this tiny mark is gradually forgotten and passes away with little significance. It is remembered by only a very few. Finally, they, too, will pass away, and all will be forgotten. The Apostle James says it clearly enough:

> *What is your life? For you are a mist that appears for a little time and then vanishes. (James 4:14)*

A simple thing, yet terribly profound—a dash on a headstone separated by two dates. Unless we know the person, now hidden from our view, it is a story that remains silent to us. But never to God. As you reflect on your own dash, what would your story be? What would it say about your life? There it is, but so quickly forgotten, *appearing for a little time and then vanishes.* The dash soon becomes just a mark on a headstone—commonplace to the casual visitor walking through the cemetery.

Yes, just a dash! That's all the space typically you are given to tell your life story. What would you want that dash to say if it were ever revealed and read by all? Just a couple of sentences might do, *if we just had the space to say it.*

Sometimes, the headstone provides a little room to capture the essence of the person's life in a few brief words: "*Now in a Better Place," "Always Serving Others,"* and the one I like, "*I Told You I Was Sick."* Some words look back. Others look forward.

Not long ago, my family had the *joyful sorrow* of placing to rest my wife's mother who passed from this life at the age of 102.

We discussed what words might be appropriate to capture the essence of Jean's life. What words could inform others about her life as they walked through the cemetery in years to come? We decided on something that characterized the life that was now, and forever, being lived: *"Rejoicing in Jesus."*

Within a few short years of Jean's passing, our family found occasion to use these same words on my wife's headstone. For us, the words so beautifully and accurately described where Beverley really is and what she is doing. But more importantly, the words reveal who she is with—*"Rejoicing in Jesus."*

Maybe such a brief statement on a headstone is all that is needed. But such words, succinct as they are, still fall short of telling the full story of what is embedded in the dash.

Maybe, the dash is all you want people to know about your life. You may think that your life story is not all that remarkable, or that the unfolding of the dash would present a story you had rather not tell.

David, king of Israel, is probably one of the most transparent characters of the Bible. In his dash nothing seems to be hidden from view. His life story from start to finish with all its failings, deceit, adultery, and murder—as well as his passion for God (see the Psalms)—is included in his fully-expanded dash. Yet, God places His eternal dash on David's headstone as recorded in Acts 13:22, *". . . I have found in David the son of Jesse a man after my heart, who will do all my will."*

Like David, if you are a new creation in Jesus Christ, God has already put His own dash on your headstone. Paul tells us in Colossians 3:3–4:

For you have died, and your life is hidden
with Christ in God.
When Christ who is your life appears,
then you also will appear with him in glory.

From David's life we learn that the only dash that counts is the one *God inscribes* on the headstone. God's dash is what the Holy Spirit has accomplished in your life and mine that brings glory to the Father through Jesus Christ. It is what God sees of Christ in you. Be it your prayers, the cup of cold water given to one in need, or your response to a Divine nudge to do His will. Whatever glorified His Son in you will be what is in your dash displayed in eternity for all to see and hear. It's really all about Him! Re-read Colossians 3:3–4.

But here we are, trying to make sense of what life is all about in the 4th quarter. Just as in David's life, our life is punctuated with a lot of up's and down's. We fail, falter, and fall. However, it is not a question of how many times we fall, but the direction we are facing when we get back up. In the game of football, the winning team always experiences failures. There may be times when they fumbled the ball, ran afoul of the umpire, violated the line of scrimmage, or missed the easy catch for the touchdown. But despite the failures, the winning team prevails because of the direction they face when they get back up—their eyes are always on the goal. *Does that describe your dash?*

As you and I consider this dash, we are faced with the same question that James asks, *"What is your life?"* The brevity of life takes on new and profound meaning when you are in the 4th quarter. The clock is ticking and intuitively we know that time is not our friend. The endgame looms before us, and our question often is, "How in the world can we ever carry the ball into the end zone?"

There is a lot packed into that little dash—the one between the two dates. Only those living *near* the end of their dash—their life on earth—fully understand all of its challenges and limitations. Next time you walk through a cemetery, consider deeply the significance of the dash:

> *"O Lord, make me know my end*
> *and what is the measure of my days;*
> *let me know how fleeting I am!*
>
> *Behold, you have made my days*
> *a few handbreadths,*
> *and my lifetime is as nothing before you.*
> *Surely all mankind stands as a mere breath! Selah*
> *(Psalm 39:4–5)*

In the next few chapters, let's see how our dash and our living life in the 4th quarter come together to help us leave a godly legacy. Remember also, that although the winning team shares in the excitement of victory, it is, ultimately, our Coach and Owner of the team that truly benefits—it is all to the praise and glory of Christ that we live and play the game. A view from the sidelines reveals much about who we are and what we will be in the 4th quarter of life—when we cross the goal line for the final time.

Wouldn't it be nice if someone who truly knew you—say God—engraved on your headstone with unfading letters, just above the dash, and just below your name, *"A Winner?"*

> *See what kind of love the Father has given to us, that we*
> *should be called children of God, and so we are . . .*
> *(I John 3:1)*

*There is therefore now no condemnation for those who are
in Christ Jesus . . . We know that for those who love God all
things work together for good, for those who are called
according to his purpose . . .*

(Romans 8:1, 28)

Let's Talk About It

1. Share with the group your observations, experiences, and reflections when you walk through a cemetery. What are some the inscriptions you remember on the headstones?

2. What is the inscription on the headstone of your loved one? Why is that important to you or to your family?

3. Having read about the *dash* between the two dates on a headstone, what personal significance does the dash *now* have for you?

4. What is the message of James 14:14 and Psalm 39:4–5 when these two references are brought together?

5. Talk about the hope that belongs to the Christian beyond the grave?

Chapter 2

What Counts – 4th Quarter Living

So if a person lives many years, let him rejoice in them all; but let him remember that the days of darkness will be many . . . (Ecclesiastes 11:8)

The journey into the 4th quarter of life usually starts well for many. They are now free to chart a new path. Theirs is a new life of hope and the fulfillment of life-long dreams. Unrestrained by the regimen, demands and unrealistic goals of the work place, they can pursue that special place to retire. Uncomplicated schedules allow for personal fulfillment and travel. These dreams for many seem to be what this new phase of life is all about.

The new reality, however, suggests otherwise. Economic and social realities paint a different picture. Increasingly, there are many who enter the 4th quarter of life with limited resources. They find they cannot realize any of these dreams. They struggle to pay the bills. Augmenting their income with continuing full or part-time employment is often not an option. Their health may decline quickly, and soon medical bills cannot be met. Keeping a roof over their head often means living *with* less and *in* less than they had before the 4th quarter. Life for them seems only to get worse. As they struggle to survive, *what counts* for them is a far different story than it is for others.

Researchers provide an outline to the stages or phases we all apparently experience, or think we should experience. We begin our lives in *innocence*. At the beginning, we probably thought we could be anyone and do most anything. We could succeed at whatever we put our hand to and live forever doing it. Soon, we enter a period of *acquisition* where the world and all it has to offer is ours, either by right or by working hard to earn it. While we are acquiring "stuff," we are hopelessly divided between work and raising a family—a time usually fraught with stress and conflict. Somewhere in our fifties and sixties we take *the stuff* we acquired and begin to *consolidate* it, learning to manage it and plan for its future use.

At last, we enter the 4th quarter of life. Here, we discover we no longer need or want *the stuff*, and we begin to *downsize*— getting rid of much of what we once believed to be a necessary part of life. Not downsizing just the material stuff, but downsizing ourselves from being hyper-busy and emotionally driven, to be more sane and simple. Here, we hope to have time to be *selective* about our activities, to *reflect peacefully* upon where our journey has brought us, and to consider what our remaining years might look like. At least that is what we may think we ought to be doing in the 4th quarter of life.

Regardless of your story, here is the reality of life in the 4th quarter. We soon realize that this final quarter of life is by far the toughest quarter of the game. In football, the fourth quarter is when the players are exhausted to their limits, when the opposing team appears the strongest. It is the time when every minute on the clock and every play coming out of the huddle is critical to reaching the goal of being a winner, of being rewarded by our Coach saying, *"Well done good and faithful servant,"* This is what every player wants to hear.

No one said it would be easy—this business of growing old. As a seasoned 4th quarter player, I know this is true in my life, as it may be in yours. I deeply sense the challenges of growing old, *or older.* In the Bible, the writer of Ecclesiastes also knew about growing old. Using colorful figurative language to describe this aging process, he says:

> *Remember also your Creator in the days of your youth, before the evil days come and the years draw near of which you will say, "I have no pleasure in them"; before the sun and the light and the moon and the stars are darkened and the clouds return after the rain, in the day when the keepers of the house tremble, and the strong men are bent, and the grinders cease because they are few, and those who look through the windows are dimmed, and the doors on the street are shut—when the sound of the grinding is low, and one rises up at the sound of a bird, and all the daughters of song are brought low—they are afraid also of what is high, and terrors are in the way; the almond tree blossoms, the grasshopper drags itself along, and desire fails, because man is going to his eternal home, and the mourners go about the streets—before the silver cord is snapped, or the golden bowl is broken, or the pitcher is shattered at the fountain, or the wheel broken at the cistern, and the dust returns to the earth as it was, and the spirit returns to God who gave it.*   *(Ecclesiastes 12:1–7)*

I am learning that growing old is part of the journey with all its trials and challenges. Although all phases of life are important, the 4th quarter is the *most* important. We often struggle with limitations, knowing we are heading quickly toward the endgame. If we are honest with ourselves, we sense increasingly that we will not be around much longer. But, getting to where we are going is sometimes the most painful part—the part that no one really likes or wants to talk about too much. Frequently, it seems to me that the process of getting old just gets in the way of living. The truth be told, however, getting old is all about living. Listen to what the Psalmist says:

> *The righteous flourish like the palm tree*
> *and grow like a cedar in Lebanon.*
> *They are planted in the house of the LORD;*
> *they flourish in the courts of our God.*
> *They still bear fruit in old age;*
> *they are ever full of sap and green,*
> *to declare that the LORD is upright;*
> *he is my rock, and there is no unrighteousness in him.*
> *(Psalm 92:12–15)*

Living life in the 4th quarter, we can be sure that the clock does not stand still. Even in our most passive and inactive moments, life is in motion, moving to a determined end. Oh yes, the heart still pumps, the blood continues to flow, and the lungs go up and down with each breath we take. But as we age, these systems also age and eventually wear out. There is not much we can do about that!

When we were younger—say in our twenties and thirties—most of us thought we were next to immortal. When we arrived in our forties, we thought we could have it all and buy our way out of any aches, pains or problems. When we got into our fifties and sixties we began to think that perhaps our thoughts of immortality were a bit premature. By the time we reached our seventies, more or less, our perceived bubble of immortality began to show signs of stress and cracking, exposing the rickety nature of our brief humanity.

We are now constantly evaluating every pain and twitching of the body in its battle against the inevitable. When getting up in the morning, if our body has two of something, one of them always seems to be hurting. We visit the doctor more often. The diagnosis is the same, "You are getting old." Although it is usually put to us in softer tones like, "Aging often brings with it these symptoms."

I think most of us arrive in the 4th quarter of life unintentionally and unremarkably. I don't remember any celebrations, no welcoming parties that in affect said, "Glad you finally made it!" Maybe for you it was when you said your final goodbyes to your co-workers, when Medicare and Social Security benefits began to show up in the mailbox, or when the idea of traveling became more about getting back home.

In the 4th quarter, you begin to experience a growing distance between what your mind says you can do and what your body says you can do. They are frequently not the same. And sometimes they just don't talk to one another. The lack of body coordination—bumping into things, dropping things—and many other events that don't work well for us, all reflect disconnects between our mind and our bodies. The time between getting up in the morning and going to bed at night seems to be less and less. Maybe you travel a couple of extra blocks "out of the way" just to cross at a signal-controlled intersection. You also may find that you start to believe the signs that say, "Beware of Dog"—risking the possibilities just isn't worth it.

One day, I looked into the mirror and saw an old man and wondered, *"Who could that be?"* That's when I really started becoming aware that I was in the 4th quarter. Afternoon naps began to feel pretty good—no, actually, afternoon naps became *a necessity!* Then, I began to notice how others, younger than me, opened doors for me and wanted to carry things to my car. "Oh, let me help you," was not an uncommon phrase. At first, I think I felt a bit offended that what they saw (me) was not capable of handling life without help. Eventually, I began to appreciate their offers to help. Oh, by the way, I don't climb ladders anymore, not even to change a light bulb. Very tempting. But I learned the hard way.

In this regard, the potential for falling is real, not just off ladders, but tripping on curbs and shallow steps. As you age, be aware of your surroundings, even if the ground is familiar, like around the house—sometimes it can be the most dangerous place. Don't even think about walking on ice! Particularly, the "black" stuff you can't see. Take your time to look where your next step is going to take you. It only takes a fraction of a second to misstep and fall. It takes a very, very long time to heal broken bones in the 4th quarter. You owe it to yourself and to others to be mindful of where you are stepping.

Also, be aware of your balance. Strange things happen in your ears as you age. The "gyro mechanism" that provides balance and stability for your body doesn't always work as well as we might like, just when we need it most. Don't assume balance. Make sure you have it when you get up from a sitting position or when you are rotating your body from one position to another. Being off balance is often a precursor to a fall. Also, do not be alarmed if your inner ear begins to make unwelcoming noise— ringing or "white noise." Things are just drying up—just 4th quarter aging.

Here are some other things we may share in common as we journey through the 4th quarter. Have you noticed that when you get together with others your age that people are less fussy about who you were in your former life? Class status and vocational distinctions between a CEO and a retail clerk just aren't all that important anymore. The fact is, that the closer we all get to the end of our dash the less these things truly matter.

Family is a big deal in the 4th quarter. We typically seek out more connectedness with our families, but we are often disappointed when they don't seem to share that same desire. Perhaps, we didn't share an emotional or physical bond in earlier years that would foster that connection. Most likely, your children are just too busy with their own families. With all the demands made upon young families—extended hours at work, managing children and their extra-curricular activities, yard and house work, community and social involvement, activities at church—there is very little time and energy left over to spend with grandpa and grandma.

From time to time, there may be an invitation to join the family in some activity. On such occasions we may be confused whether we are part of the family, or just "another suitcase." We may receive an occasional phone call, email or text—maybe even a Skype visit. But these encounters usually offer less than what we expect. In our present culture, we apparently want more than is rightfully ours—time with our family. Often we sense we are alone! Blessed are you if this is not the case in your experience.

For better or worse, we are inseparably tied to our families. Whether we want to be or intend to be, we become increasingly more dependent on them for many life issues— climbing ladders; heavy lifting; cutting the grass; consultation; and, eventually, managing our finances. But in our day of family brokenness, we find the reverse also may be true. Our families are dependent on us.

Many families today are made up of messy problems that still require much from us, as parents, to sort out. In many cases, our families need our care, guidance and support. What we thought we left behind in a previous stage of life is demanding more from us. This often only compounds the challenges of *living life in the 4th quarter.*

Grief is part of *living life in the 4th quarter.* We may not want to think about it too hard or too long, but if you are a couple, one of you will typically depart this life before the other— sometime in the 4th quarter. One of you will experience the grief of loss and aloneness. How you cope and how you manage your grief is important to your own well-being. When the loss first occurs, you probably will be too busy to notice grief. But it will come, sometimes in waves of thought and emotion. At other times, it may be just a word, a thought, something that was said by someone or a visual image. Any of these can trigger a thought of grief and a sense of loss. If you are having problems dealing with your grief, seek out professional help. There is also excellent literature on the subject of managing your grief and loneliness.

Our adventure in the 4th quarter of life will be told differently by each of us. And yet, common to all, will be the overwhelming issues and consuming demands that challenge our lives. But, *there is still a life to be lived. That's what counts in the 4th quarter.*

Let's Talk About It

1. Okay, so now you are retired. What are some of your challenges and opportunities you have as a *member* of the 4th quarter? How are your friends doing with this business of growing old? What are their challenges?

2. How are medical issues limiting what you would like to do with your life? Explain the word GRIT as you face these 4th quarter problems.

3. Family is always a big part of 4th quarter living. How would you describe your present relationship with your family? How are they helping you to adjust to this new phase of life? How much do you still need to "parent" them?

4. Have you had to deal with grief from the loss of a loved one? What are the impacts of this grief upon you life? What are you doing to *manage* grief? How are others helping?

5. *Ecclesiastes 12:1–7* is a very graphic picture of what happens to us when we grow old. Interpret the images the writer uses as they apply to the limitations that come as we age. List them. Talk about them!

Chapter 3

Old Players – Still in the Game

Two are better than one, because they have a good reward
for their toil. For if they fall, one will lift up his fellow. But woe to
him who is alone when he falls and has not another to lift him up!
(Ecclesiastes 4:9–10)

We have all seen it—the picture of "Harry and Mary" growing old together. Happily, they venture off into their sunset years of "eternal" bliss. Together they enjoy a wonderful problem-free life of shared happiness, contentment, and love. The only problem with this picture is that Harry and Mary usually don't live where the rest of us live.

Certainly, the beginning of our 4th quarter can be a wonderful experience of togetherness—depending, of course, on how well the previous quarters have gone. Assuming all went well, these early 4th quarter years are very productive. Doing together many things for the first time—things like travel, gardening, volunteer work, playing golf, etc., all can be enjoyed as a couple. All these "together" things help build a deeper relationship and a closer bonding between one another. Fewer of life's distractions are around to bother us. This allows us time to focus on each other. But unhappily this "happily-ever-after" story does not last.

Soon, 4th quarter issues begin to emerge. Usually they are health issues—initially not serious. But in time they become more acute and even chronic. Thankfully, as a couple, one person can help the other. Isn't that what being married is all about—helping one another? "Togetherness" can and should go on. However, shared activities, hopes, and dreams become more limited. Maybe, it means sitting on the couch together to enjoy past memories from an old photo album. Maybe, traveling together means a night visiting some distant land from a library video. Maybe, it's a quiet evening spent with friends to play cards or just to talk about the good old days—you know, when life *seemed* more simple. However, the time of togetherness that was once taken for granted, now becomes more intentional, more managed, and more uncertain.

Then, it happens. In time, both spouses are dealing with long-term serious ailments, making each incapable of truly helping the other. Or, as is often the case, the 4th quarter is over for one of the team members—our spouse dies. Family, friends or health services are soon needed.

A spouse is seriously afflicted with a deteriorating disease such as cancer or dementia. Life becomes less of a partnership and more about caregiving and receiving care. The inevitable overwhelms the relationship. Giving care consumes every minute of the day. Usually, the ailing spouse is placed into a care facility and the once viable partnership is shattered. The other spouse is left to face life *almost* alone. This subject is more fully described in my book, *This Ugly Disease – A Caregiver's Journey into Pain, Anguish and Hope* (2016; Available at www.amazon.com). Where are *Harry and Mary* when you need them?

Eventually, at the end of the dash, one or the other spouse is left to manage life in the 4th quarter alone—really alone! If you are the one left alone, remember the clock is still ticking; and the game is still in play. No matter how tough or apparently impossible life becomes, it is not over until *you* hear, *"Well done good and faithful servant."* But there are some things you can do to help your situation.

When you are *growing old together,* plan together. Face the reality that neither of you are going to live forever. One will probably die before the other. Together, prepare for that day. Proverbs (Proverbs 30:24–25) talks about ants that being wise prepared for the winter by gathering food during the summer. As ants, prepare for the hard times while you are still enjoying the summer—the good years together.

Together, deal specifically and honestly about your future. Prepare for the *hard times* in a way that both of you fully understand your situation. Lay out a written plan for your finances, living accommodations, family arrangements, legal documents (wills, trusts), advanced health directives, interment arrangements, etc. Do this in the "good years." Don't be surprised and unprepared when the day of being alone is handed to you. This day will come, and it will arrive during the 4th quarter of life.

During the good years, talk candidly with your family about your plans for the *hard times.* Don't let the conversation be dismissed as unimportant or irrelevant. Your family's ability and willingness to engage with you at this level of conversation will say a lot about how transparent your relationship was with them in previous years.

Maybe a *Harry* or a *Mary* is coming into the 4th quarter alone, living solo, as people who have never been married or perhaps with a spouse who died in a previous quarter. Being prepared is no less important for you than those with a living spouse. The challenges of this quarter may be different and unique. However, all of the elements mentioned above apply: finances, living accommodations, family arrangements, legal documents (wills, trusts), advanced health directives, interment arrangements, etc., need to be settled as you enter the 4th quarter of life.

If there are no immediate family or trusted friends to discuss and help with these matters, then consulting a life-management service may be an option for making appropriate arrangements. Regardless of who it is, you will need someone to represent you in the 4th quarter and with end-of-life affairs. Seek out other single people your age to see how they are handling these questions. Don't put off the realities of the 4th quarter until you are physically or mentally unable to deal with these issues. Remember, it doesn't matter whether you are married or single. *You are still in the game. Don't quit before the game is over.*

Now, if you are still curious about *Harry and Mary*, follow their continuing adventures in the next issue of *Senior Living* magazine.

Let's Talk About It

1. Togetherness is a beautiful thing. What are some of the activities you and your spouse do together? How often do you do them? Do you both enjoy doing them?

2. What kind of plans have you and your spouse made in anticipation that one of you will be incapable of making life-important decisions in the future? How are you, or your spouse, prepared to handle what is required to be a caregiver?

3. Have you brought your family into your plans? Is someone designated to assume *power of attorney* and make decisions on your behalf? Are there family problems regarding these decisions?

4. Have you, together, made prior interment arrangements— funeral home, cemetery, etc.? If not, why not?

Chapter 4

Playing The Game Well

I have fought the good fight, I have finished the race,
have kept the faith. (2 Timothy 4:7)

Every player on the team, no matter what their position, wants to play well. They are investing every resource they have, every bit of training they have received, and every ounce of strength and perseverance they can muster to win the game. Having navigated into the uncertain waters of the 4th quarter, I have gained some insights that are helping me push toward the goal. I would like to pass them on to you. But first, a comment.

There are some folks who arrive at the 4th quarter of life thinking the game is over—that the game only has three quarters. They lounge comfortably in front of the TV, protect their domain from unwanted intrusions (maybe with a *Rottweiler* or *pit bull*), and, generally, try to let the time on the clock run out. However they view themselves, they are not in the game from God's perspective. They have not finished fighting the good fight. They are on the sidelines watching the game go by.

If we are to stay in the game and play as winners, if we are to hear, *"Well done good and faithful servant,"* we need to embrace the things that will help us get to the goal line. For some, this may be easy. For most, it comes with great difficultly and cost. Putting game-winning values into our lives is hard and challenging work, especially in the 4th quarter of life. It must be done with stubborn determination. Here, then, are some insights I have picked up along the way:

Make Friends

Having friends is critical in our final stage of life. Fourth-quarter living can be very lonely, even for a couple without friends. Here, I am talking *not* about people we know as contacts from our phone directory, acquaintances from work, clubs or church, or even the many "friends" we collect on Facebook.

The people I am speaking about are those with whom we have bonded over time, with whom we have forged a common path—emotionally, physically, and spiritually. These are people with whom we share genuine life experiences that are sustainable and unbreakable. Although our spouse may be *our best friend*, I am talking about others woven into the fabric of our lives.

These are friends with whom we share a deep respect and steadfast appreciation. This kind of bonding doesn't seem to be bothered by great distances or lapses of time. Making up for lost time is usually not needed. It picks up where it left off. This is the kind of friendship that needs to be nourished and protected in the 4th quarter. True friends sound a lot like I Corinthians 13:4–7:

> *Love is patient and kind; love does not envy or*
> *boast; it is not arrogant or rude. It does not insist*
> *on its own way; it is not irritable or resentful; it*
> *does not rejoice at wrongdoing, but rejoices with*
> *the truth. Love bears all things, believes all things,*
> *hopes all things, endures all things.*

There are a growing number of lonely people in the 4th quarter. They are coming up short of true friends. They never bothered investing in long-term relationships when they were younger. They have contacts, but not friendships. Most of our business or ministry life has been about developing networks of people. These networks are usually not much more than value-added associations. Sadly, we spent our time identifying and nurturing contacts rather than cultivating sustainable relationships—true and durable friendships that are good for a lifetime.

Most of us are agenda-driven people who are not oriented toward embracing people as a value. This is an affliction that is pervasive in many western cultures. I have neighbors who are from India. If it were not for them, I would still have other neighbors that are strangers. This Indian couple values people and cultivates relationships by having a few of us to gather occasionally and share a meal at their table. Why? Because friends are important to them—people matter to them. They embrace that value. The rest of us can learn something from them.

Agendas are rarely the soil that produces relationships that will be with you when you are 70, 80 or 90 years old. With cell phones, Facebook and Twitter, people today have plenty of contacts and "friends." However, few of us are willing to invest time *off-line* and put forth the effort to build lasting relationships. Few want to commit to another person at the level a friendship requires. We can talk in general about *all* of our "friends," while remaining desperately alone—alone, without a true soul mate.

For most of us, building friendships isn't high on our list of priorities. It takes work. It takes mutual resolve and commitment, two things largely lacking in our culture today. We seem too focused on "me" and "mine." We hesitate to be too involved in another person's life. We would rather avoid taking the risks and assuming the costs that these kinds of friendships often require.

These kinds of relationships require time to nurture. Don't be in a hurry! It requires sacrifice. It will personally cost you something to build and grow relationships that endure.

41

These relationships require involvement in someone else's life—physically, emotionally, and spiritually. They require that you be openly honest, candid, and vulnerable. Although true friends are rare, I would stress that they are extremely important to us in the final quarter of life. *Go out and grow some friends!* There is still a place and time to make wonderful friendships during our journey in the 4th quarter.

Many of us seem to be busy going somewhere. As we hurry along, I am afraid we overlook the growing number of people in our community who are going nowhere. They are just waiting—waiting for someone to call, visit or take somewhere—someone who might become a friend. Family can neglect or forget the loneliness of their senior members, even those in their own homes. Yes, loneliness is real and it affects many older people. *Friends are so important for them—and for us!*

The most underdeveloped and under-cultivated friendship we have is the one with Jesus—one that is always available. As our friend, He has already committed Himself completely to us:

> *Greater love has no one than this, that someone lay down his life for his friends. You are my friends if you do what I command you. No longer do I call you servants, for the servant does not know what his master is doing; but I have called you friends, for all that I have heard from my Father I have made known to you. (John 15:13–15)*

To rekindle our friendship with Jesus may be harder in the 4th quarter. Life seems rigid and less open to spiritual realities. We may become cynical, argumentative and frustrated with the Church—*and with God*. We can become angry with our physical and emotional limitations, with the lack of attention and interaction with our families, etc.

We need to be disciplined and deliberate in nurturing our relationship with Jesus. He is our Lord, for sure; but He is also our friend. Not only does our friendship with Him need to be nurtured, it must become contagious. We may agree that people need God. Yes! But, *people also need people.* You and I are the hands and feet, *the smile and words* of Jesus in this 4th quarter of life to others—our spouse, families and friends—to everyone who God puts in our path to bless, *today!*

Be Kind to Your Body and Mind

Exercising is something that doesn't excite me. It is at the bottom of my preferred "to do" list. At 102 my mother-in-law, Jean, still exercised each morning with great enthusiasm. Although limited by two hip replacements, a fractured pelvic bone and a walker, she was committed to exercising. As a younger woman, she was an amateur ice-skating speed racer, a pitcher on a woman's baseball team, as well as a strong relay swimmer. She embraced the experience and knew the benefits of *daily* exercise, even at an older age—to the very end of the game!

Although I do not embrace the experience, I know the benefits of daily exercise. Inactivity in the 4th quarter of life is your worst enemy. Without it, the body quickly becomes rigid, and, like a potato chip, very brittle. This leads to all sorts of unwanted physical problems, and quite possibly to frequent trips to the doctors—and maybe to the hospital.

Keep physically active with a regimen of exercise. Working in the yard, although good, is not the same. Working out at a local gym, swimming, playing tennis, walking, and playing golf (as long as you don't get stressed playing the game)—all are good. If your balance is good, ride your bike, skate or go dancing. Keep at it even though you may need to adjust the type and length of exercise you do as you get older. Many gyms feature a group exercise program called *Silver Sneakers*. This program is for those who as less able. Disciplined exercise is a requirement in the 4th quarter.

Mandy Oaklander, health writer for Time Magazine, suggests we get at least 150–minutes a week of moderate intensity (low impact) cardio-exercise. She says new research reveals that even a small of amount of physical activity will "trigger dozens of beneficial changes in the body." Some of these benefits include 1) greater benefit for your brain which may help to deflect, not cure, the onset of Alzheimer's disease); 2) promote a happier you; 3) slow the aging process; and 4) make your skin look better. Regular exercise also 5) improves your heart function; 6) lowers the blood sugar level (good for diabetic conditions); 7) helps in the recovery from major illness and surgeries when combined with appropriate therapies; and 8) shrinks fat cells. *All good stuff!*

Not being the pacesetter for exercising, I am committed to do my part. I start with a morning exercise routine that includes 15–minutes of stretching all parts of the body. I do this daily. In addition, every other day I do a 20–minute low-impact cardio exercise. When the weather is conducive, a daily 20–minute energized walk around the neighborhood completes my routine. Be innovative, but do it. Good advice from one who does not like to exercise. The benefits are obvious! But the sad statistic is that only 20 percent are getting the exercise they need for playing the game well in the 4th quarter.

Jean also believed in exercising her mind. She was a whiz at math, doing in her head what most of us depend on our handheld calculator to do for us. She was an avid reader and a genius at crossword puzzles. She also enjoyed thought-provoking conversations about theology, philosophy and politics. Each day she set aside a quiet time. She spent that time reading the Bible and praying. Strengthening her faith was an integral part of Jean's exercise program.

Unfortunately, we live in a day when our thumbs and fingers are exercised the most. In sending texts, tweets and Facebook messages to our "friends", we move our fingers deftly over the keyboard of our smart phones an average of 15 different times an hour. I recently saw six young people gathering in a park. I thought they were gathering to talk to one another. However, it turned out to be a gathering of silence! Each had their cell phone, and was busily conversing to someone without actually saying a word—maybe texting each other *via* their cell phones?

I have also seen some older people like that—consumed with their cell phones at public events. Whatever they were doing with their cell phone appeared to be unrelated to the event they were attending. I'm not sure they could tell you what the event was about. They were in a different world!

One of my favorite computer images is one showing the day the family came to visit Grandma. There they are, about eight of them comfortably sitting on a big semi-circular living room sofa, with the grandchildren on the floor, immediately in front of the sofa. Grandma is sitting on the sofa in the middle of her family. So far so good. But here is where the picture reveals our culture. Each of the eight family members is on their cell phone—texting. Grandma is sitting there, *alone*, with a quizzical look on her face. You can fill in the blank as to what Grandma is thinking. The caption reads, *A Visit with Grandma.*

Real conversation is slipping away from us. As we spend more time on our smart phones, computers or sitting in front of the TV, we end up spending less time in *real* conversation with others, *even our spouses*. Research has shown that excessive use of cell phones and TV has a direct effect on our minds. Our brains are becoming lethargic, de-sensitized and numbed—less able to connect with the *real* world around us. Blood circulation is also affected, leading to all sorts of problems. Keep engaging people, not a screen!

Allow me to throw some paint on the canvas of your life. Exercise your mind with challenging *cognitive* activities. Watching TV is not one of them. Read, do crossword puzzles, get involved with extended learning classes, participate in clubs or volunteer work, learn new computer skills, engage in a hobby like gardening (not just by digging holes and putting seeds in the ground, but as an involved nurturer, an expert gardener), and get with others who will challenge you to think. Meditate and pray (go outdoors and clear the cobwebs from your sleepy mind). Become a student of the Bible; write a book *(sure you can!)*. Stay connected to the life of your church and your community. Embrace change. Be curious about everything! *Remember, without curiosity we would all still be living by candlelight.*

Eating properly is just as important for our age as exercising. Plain and simple—our metabolism has changed. We are getting older. For most of us, eating is different now than it used to be. Our bodies are going to react badly if we eat how and what we ate in years past. More digestive problems, more weight gain—these are the realities of eating like we used to. Everything you are trying to achieve through exercising will be undone. You will add pounds, feel sluggish, and boost your blood sugar levels above where they need to be. That means you will be a candidate for diabetes. Forget about diet plans—they really don't work for the long haul.

To help you get started on a new and lasting approach to eating like you should, I recommend getting a book written by Dennis Pollock, *60 Ways to Lower Your Blood Sugar: Simple Steps to Reduce the Carbs, Shed Weight, and Feel Great Now!* (Harvest House Publishers, 2013). I check my blood pressure two or three times a week at home or at my local drug store. I also get periodic blood tests for my blood sugar and cholesterol levels. Just be sure to see your doctor regularly. Tell him or her about your plan for a healthier you. They should be excited to help.

Engage both your body and your mind in exercise. Why do some people at 90 and above appear to be alert, astute and active, while others seem unsure as to what side of the grave they are on from day to day? Though, our genes can be an important factor in how our mind and body behave after 90, being active is critical, even when serious limitations of aging creep up on us. *Remember Jean!*

Laugh a Lot More

I find that a lot of older folks seem to have forgotten how to laugh. Many have lost their sense of humor. Not much is funny anymore! Things look pretty grim most of the time—*like the six-o'clock news.*

Thinking back, our house was filled with laughter. Jean and Bev found something to laugh at most every day. According to medical research, laughter is good for our minds and our bodies. It relieves stress and resets reality. We need to do more laughing—not "silly" laughing but sincere laughing. As we age, we do dumb things, at least I do. I need to remind myself not to be angry or frustrated with these things, not to take myself too seriously. I am learning to laugh at them, at least with a quiet chuckle. I'm sure God does!

Getting together friends whose laughter is contagious will, in time, infect us as well. Curiously, the Bible frequently speaks about being joyful, rejoicing and singing as *commands.* These behaviors don't seem to be optional, even in the 4th quarter.

Many times, Jesus and the Apostles tell us to be joyful and rejoice, and, of course, to be thankful. Instead, I find many older people complaining, being angry and unthankful. With the final goal line in view, shouldn't we who know we are winners sing, rejoice, and laugh a lot more? Life in the 4th quarter will be a lot easier if you adopt this attitude and behavior. And, you will feel a lot better.

Stay Flexible

Rubber is a very flexible substance, except when it gets old or has not been cared-for. It then becomes brittle and breakable. Getting old in the 4th quarter can be a lot like old rubber—rubber that is not properly cared-for. Old rubber becomes useless for the job it was intended to do.

As we age, we can become very rooted in our ways of behaving and thinking. Rigidity sets in—like old rubber. We can become pessimistic, sarcastic, and distrustful. We can assume we are "right" and everyone else is "wrong." We are more inclined to argue than to be reasonable.

We don't like our plans to be changed. We see change as "bad." But as we engage our world, including planning times with our families, we find that change is what most of life is about. One of the most challenging things about life in the 4th quarter is being willing to change as we age—staying flexible.

Life is about change! Everything does, except God. He is unchanging, perfect in the absolute. Nothing in our life is perfect. Whether it involves schedules, plans, or situations, let's agree that life never will be perfect this side of heaven. I am finding that the things I resist most don't really matter that much. So, why should I be concerned or upset about change when things don't go right? Aim for a humble and supple spirit, free from cynicism, arguing and complaining.

Here's what I am learning. I do not always have to be right—*God still calls the shots*. One time, while debating an unclear theological point, a pastor, who was much older than I at the time, told me that I could be wrong, and he could be right. Or, he could be wrong, and I could be right. Or, we both could be wrong!

Actually, there is a certain satisfaction in knowing that others can be right, and I could be wrong. When I realize that I am wrong it means I am still capable of learning new things. Jean always welcomed the opportunity to learn new things—to have her mind challenged and changed. Embrace change and don't be upset when it comes. *God is still at work in your life!*

Growing old is something I don't need to resist or fight. It's all part of life. Those of us in the 4th quarter can truly enjoy the freedom and flexibility of growing old, if we set our mind to it. *It's all about attitude!*

Don't be easily angered. I have learned that most fits of anger (even road rage) are indicators of immaturity. And, such anger leads to sin, ultimately against God. If we believe that God is sovereign, then we should learn to be patient, even quiet. He controls everything from the smallest particle in the atom to the far reaches of the universe. If I am angry with others, God, or myself, what do I believe about His sovereignty—His love, mercy and plan for my life? Short-lived anger—defined as *righteous indignation*—may at times be necessary. But never go to bed with it (Ephesians 4:26–27). Remember, our behavior reflects what we *truly* believe about God. He is in control!

As we get older and continue to lose both our flexibility and our ability to handle change, one day our physical body, our mind, or both, may become a source of embarrassment to us. That's okay! It's just our life slowly perishing—remember that we are but *a mist, a vapor that is vanishing.* This is good medicine for any lingering elements of pride. Someday, we may be wearing diapers (again) in a wheelchair in an assisted living or memory care facility. Others will need to feed us, wash us and see to our toilet needs. How's that for needing to be flexible!

As we get to the end of our dash, the mind can cause us to do and say things we would normally find unacceptable and, maybe, even reprehensible. We may have been a "saint" in previous years, but now have a vocabulary that could shock a sailor on shore leave. Our previous lives may have appeared as peaceful as a placid lake. However, now they exhibit anger and agitation beyond recognition. And, there may be other behaviors that normally would be viewed as shameful. Remember, this does not surprise God. He is still in control. For us, crossing the goal line for the final time will still be joyful. Still, if it is within our power to control, we should never let our spiritual life become an embarrassment to us, to our family, or to our friends.

Forgive—Do It!

Some people in the 4th quarter of life don't let go. Holding a grudge has imprisoned their life. Something that someone said or did became *unforgiveable.* Their grudge will only be buried when they are. They never get over it. They never let go of it. By not *giving* forgiveness, which is always in their power to do, they condemn themselves to a life of bitterness that affects their spirit, mind, and body. The Scripture is very clear about what we should do:

> *I say to you, "Love your enemies and pray for those who persecute you, so that you may be sons of your Father who is in heaven...."* (Matthew 5:44–45)

> *...if one has a complaint against another, forgiving each other; as the Lord has forgiven you, so you also must forgive.* (Colossians 3:13)

Little commentary is needed. Forgiveness is a command, not an option, not a situational preference. When someone has really hurt you, how are you to respond? *...as the Lord has forgiven you*—unconditionally! Where would you and I be if God said I will only forgive you *if*—or if He chose, not to forgive at all? Not forgiving is our greatest sin. But...

> *If we confess our sins, he is faithful and just to forgive us our sins and to cleanse us from all unrighteousness.* (I John 1:9)

Not allowing ourselves to be forgiven is just as bad. If we refuse *forgiveness* from others or from God—or do not forgive ourselves for some infraction, failure, or neglect—then we need to refer again to Colossians 3:13. This is a command, and, as before, you need to do it unconditionally. Not allowing ourselves to be forgiven is a sin. A sin to be confessed—a sin to be forgiven. Refusing forgiveness is to demean and dismiss the power of the cross—the truth about God's love, which always holds out forgiveness. Remember, it's not a perfect world. God's forgiveness allows for that.

Keep Focused

We have all experienced going into a room for something, but, once arriving, we find we have forgotten why we are there. Or, we might be in the middle of a conversation and forget where we are going with our next thought. In the 4th quarter, this quirk of forgetfulness may show up more often than we would like. Don't be alarmed. First of all, laugh at it. Don't be angry or stressed by it. That does not help us.

Whether you are walking, driving or talking, staying focused may become increasingly difficult. But paying attention may keep you safe! Be deliberate in your thinking. Don't allow your mind to wander by being distracted with other thoughts or by what you see or hear along the way. If need be, and as appropriate, carry on a running conversation with yourself en route about where you are going and what you are going to do when you get there. Also, consider making a little note to yourself and carrying it with you so that when you arrive you can refer to it to know why you are *there*. All this takes time and a special effort. Welcome to the 4th quarter!

Focus in the 4th quarter also means paying attention to the really important stuff. As we get older, the list of truly important stuff should get shorter. Even now, I sense I spend too much time focusing on the non-essentials—things that are just not all that important to the outcome of the game. With diminishing resources, staying focused will keep your feet on the ground and your eyes on the goal.

Maintain a Passion For Life and For God

People coming into the 4th quarter bring with them different life-interests. For some it is golf, tennis, cycling or other physical activity. For others, it is travel, gardening, volunteer work, photography, painting, or writing. In the community where I live, there are about a dozen special events each month. In addition, there are nearly 100 clubs or groups one could join. Each of these activities offers a certain expression and passion for life.

As I look around, I see others who seemingly have no passion for much of anything. For them, life seems to be focused within a very tight circle, mostly *them*. From their perspective, not even God really cares about them all that much. At the end of their lives, they have lost the meaning and the joy of life. Each new day is not much different than the one before. Simply, they are bored with life. They have forgotten that *"the chief end of man is to glorify God and to enjoy Him forever."* Unhappily, the joy of the Lord is no longer part of their daily experience.

In a newly published book, *Move Toward the Mess*, *The Ultimate Fix for a Boring Christian Life*, written by John Hambrick (David Cook, 2016), the author makes an appeal to fix a boring Christian life by getting involved with messes. One comes to mind—the Good Samaritan (Luke 10:30–37). Choosing compassion over convenience, embracing interruptions over well-planned agendas, and going deep into the messes all around us is a sure way to relieve boredom. Moving toward the messes in people's lives is costly. It means time and treasure—the price of fixing boredom. Jesus was never boring nor should we be. The way to fix a boring 4th quarter life is to move toward the messes in people's lives—in our families, friends, neighbors, and whoever we meet along the way. With wisdom and prayer, each of us can do that.

This requires that we be involved with life, embracing life's issues as they cross our paths. Not by being overwhelmed by them, but by saying, "Here is a problem; let's see how we are going to fix it." Make a plan to reach out to others in need, using your own personal contacts or those available through your church or civic organizations.

Here it is in Scripture:

Never be lacking in zeal, but keep your spiritual fervor, serving the Lord. Be joyful in hope, patient in affliction, faithful in prayer. Share with God's people who are in need. Practice hospitality. *(Romans 12:11–13)*

We who are in the 4th quarter of life have many wonderful opportunities to move toward people with messy lives. We can help alleviate many of these problems with our time, talent and treasure. Avoid a dull, uninteresting, and boring life by being passionate for the things God is passionate about—*people!* We are never too old, nor are we ever too limited by our situation to be moving toward the messes in order to advance God's kingdom agenda.

My wife, Beverley, spent the last eight months of her life with dementia in a memory care facility. Yet, even in her declining condition, she kept an outward focus on helping people who could not help themselves. Routinely, she would help feed people at mealtime who were unable to feed themselves—people who had bigger messes than she had. For her, being outwardly passionate began with her heart not with her mind.

We need to continually stoke the fire of passion for life. Embrace it, engage it, and enjoy it. This is particularly true in the 4th quarter when detractors will come and tell you that such a pursuit is for younger blood. A passion for life is an attitude of continuing pursuit. It will shape our endgame and help us finish as the winners we are. Dream big dreams and pursue them. *You don't have much time!*

A desire for God is another passion that is often missing in the later years of life. Placing Him at *the head of the table* is a must. Only then will life be fulfilling. Fourth quarter living is not a time for retirement from God. As a friend of mine says, "It is a time for *re-firement, not retirement.*" We may have been active in ministry in the past, but we never retire from ministry. We never retire from following Jesus. Venues may change, the direction may be different, but Jesus still says, "Follow Me." Even in old age, we are to follow closely—close enough to be covered by the dust from His sandals.

This is the last quarter of life on earth. The final goal is in view. Don't fumble the ball! Play hard to the end. Be faithful to the One who called you. Maintain a deep and abiding relationship with Him as "friend with friend." It may seem that our passion for God wanes with the passing of time. But keep focused. If we are to hear *"well done good and faithful servant,"* then God must be in first place—the only place that will remain as other passions and desires fall away. One day He will be our *only* passion, our *only* desire.

> *"One holy passion filling all my frame . . . "*
> *(From, Spirit of God, Descend upon My Heart, by George Croly, 1780–1860)*
>
> *One thing have I asked of the Lord, that will I seek after: that I may dwell in the house of the Lord all the days of my life, to gaze upon the beauty of the Lord and to inquire in his temple. (Psalm 27:4)*

Let's Talk About It

1. There are many things that will help your body, mind, and soul engage in activities, attitudes, and behaviors that keep the "wheels of your wagon" all going in the right direction in the 4th quarter. Which of those mentioned in this chapter do you benefit most from? Why?

2. What other things can you add to the list? How do they work for you?

3. Why is keeping passionate for God more difficult in our older years? What can you do to improve your passion for God? Why is passion for God important?

4. Discuss *Romans 12:11–13*. How do these verses work for 4th quarter people? In these verses, what things are most challenging? What can you do to improve in these areas? Be specific!

∞∞

We have covered a lot of ground and discussed many things that touch our lives when thinking about *living life in the 4th quarter*. We walked through the cemetery and saw our *dash*, marking the journey between our birth and death. We each have one, and one day it will be where all can see it. One day, God will open it for all of heaven to read.

We took a journey into our 4th quarter. We looked at what counts among the many things that don't. We looked at some of the most common issues we face during this last stage of life. Although the issues may vary in intensity they are all common to our experience.

We considered what it means to grow old together as a couple, and when the death of a spouse leaves us alone. We also looked at what it means to come into the 4th quarter alone, living solo.

Lastly, we considered some things I found helpful in my 4th quarter: make friends, be kind to your body and mind, laugh a lot more, stay flexible, forgive, keep focused and maintain a passion for life and God.

Remember, the 4th quarter of life is a time of preparation, not a conclusion. The Bible stresses the need to be ready and to prepare, not only for this life, but also for the life to come. You cannot undo the past, but you can *wisely* engage the future. The 4th quarter of life is a God-given moment for you to prepare! Use it!

In our next chapter, we will consider how to *leave a godly legacy*—a perspective that may revolutionize how you live your life in the 4th quarter.

Chapter 5

Final Score – Leaving A Godly Legacy

"When your children ask their fathers in times to come, 'What do these stones mean?' then you shall let your children know . . . that the hand of the LORD is mighty, that you may fear the LORD your God forever. (Joshua 21, 24)

Most of us want to leave something from our lives for the next generation. Something significant—a final score that wins the game! In the minds of many that usually means leaving something material for our children. Unless we are blessed with material wealth, most of us will leave little in that regard. Our families will probably not get rich from our legacy. At best, maybe there is a small insurance policy or some real estate. But we can still leave a godly legacy. This is a legacy that has value far beyond material wealth. As we will see, it is never too late to begin leaving a godly legacy.

I grew up in a family that was average by the standards of that time. My sister, brother and I grew up in a loving, caring family with no divorces—how different is that! My father worked hard and, at times, long hours. We never lacked what we needed. Mother worked outside the home, but only during the War years (World War II). We always had the knowledge that mom, for the most part, would be home if we needed her.

My sister, brother, and I wanted to hear stories about our family that came before us. But, no one then living knew much about what went on before them. I guess no one from our past family felt that it was important enough to share memories with the younger generation. In effect, we had no stones . . . *almost.*

Obviously, when my father and mother passed away, the material part they left behind was small, indeed. But, there was one small stone—a memorial stone that was left behind. It was a Bible that belonged to my grandfather. As a young boy I remember that Bible. It was buried deep in a closet. No one read it or referred to it. One day I found it and began to read it, with no understanding of its real message. But it was the beginning of my spiritual journey.

Through many twists and turns, I eventually came to a personal faith in Jesus Christ. With the passing of years, married and with a family, I began the laborious task of building a "memorial of stones" that one day will serve as a legacy for my family and to theirs, hopefully for generations to come.

Dinnertime in our home was typically a two-hour event. Besides eating a delicious meal, we learned to talk and share. Interaction was encouraged as each member of the family told about their day. It was not a formal event, but one where engagement was expected. I would include a short reading from the Bible, collectively shared from an age-appropriate book usually with a missions theme, read missionary letters and play table games. There was no requirement to stay at the table for two hours, but most of the family did. This, along with bedtime activities, was how I built a memorial of stones for my family. Did I do it perfectly? No. But I wanted a legacy for my children. Here is what God said to the prophet Isaiah about just such a legacy:

As for me, this is my covenant with them," says the LORD. "My Spirit, who is on you, will not depart from you, and my words that I have put in your mouth will always be on your lips, on the lips of your children and on the lips of their descendants—from this time on and forever," says the LORD. (Isaiah 59:21, NIV)

In the Bible, I find that God is very concerned about stones—memorials that would speak to future generations. Stones that would speak about who God is and all that He has done in redeeming us—so we would not forget. Whether stones, or some bread and a cup of wine at the communion table—all speak of His greatness and mercy in redeeming His people.

And those twelve stones, which they took out of the Jordan, Joshua set up at Gilgal. And he said to the people of Israel, "When your children ask their fathers in times to come, 'What do these stones mean?' then you shall let your children know, 'Israel passed over this Jordan on dry ground.' For the LORD your God dried up the waters of the Jordan for you until you passed over, as the LORD your God did to the Red Sea, which he dried up for us until we passed over, so that all the peoples of the earth may know that the hand of the LORD is mighty, that you may fear the LORD your God forever." (Joshua 4:20-24)

For believers in Jesus Christ, a godly legacy is our stones—our memorial stones. Just as we have seen with the dash, the stones represent our life story about God transforming our lives through Christ. These stones also speak of what He has accomplished in and through our lives—all for His glory. This is the story my family needs to hear. It's the only one that truly matters in the end—the only one that will remain when everything else is forgotten.

This story is simple in its appearance and presentation, but profound in its impact upon those who receive it. The sum of your life is what God is using to glorify Himself. The Apostle Paul says it well in Philippian 2:9-11.

> *Therefore God has highly exalted him and bestowed on him the name that is above every name, so that at the name of Jesus every knee should bow, in heaven and on earth and under the earth, and every tongue confess that Jesus Christ is Lord, to the glory of God the Father.*

He wants His story to be told, and only you can do it. This is your godly legacy. This is the story about Jesus Christ in you who is our hope of glory. These are the stones to be passed on to the next generation, and to the next, and to the ones that will follow. Your legacy is the story of your life. But it is more than the people, experiences, values, and philosophy that shaped it. Central to your story is Jesus Christ, the one who is *still* shaping your life for His glory. The one you are *still* following. This is the real legacy story about God and how His redemptive faithfulness has been interwoven throughout the fabric of your life.

You might say, "My story is not all that interesting, and probably not that important. Why bother?" Here's what God says about the story of your life . . .

> *Give ear, O my people, to my teaching; incline your ears to the words of my mouth! I will open my mouth in a parable; I will utter dark sayings from of old, things that we have heard and known, that our fathers have told us. We will not hide them from their children, but tell to the coming generation the glorious deeds of the Lord, and his might, and the wonders that he has done. (Psalms 78:1-4)*

Your legacy is important because God is important. Your story is *His* story. Over the years, God has been investing His eternal love, mercy and faithfulness in your life through Jesus Christ. It is a story that needs to be told to your children and to theirs. Throughout the remaining years of your life, your story needs to be told and deposited into the lives of your children, their children, and to others who care to listen.

> He established a testimony in Jacob and appointed a law in Israel, which he commanded our fathers to teach to their children, that the next generation might know them, the children yet unborn, and arise and tell them to their children, so that they should set their hope in God and not forget the works of God, but keep his commandments . . . (Psalm 78:5-7)

> O God, from my youth you have taught me, and I still proclaim your wondrous deeds. So even to old age and gray hairs, O God, do not forsake me, until I proclaim your might to another generation, your power to all those to come. (Psalms 71:17-18)

We live in a time when the family "teaching pulpit" largely no longer exists. Most of us in the 4th quarter can remember when evening supper, or dinner, was a daily event that brought together the whole family, not just to eat, but to share what was going on in the life of the family—at school, at work, or around the house. It was also a time when the head of the family, usually the father, read the Bible, prayed, and share something about what God was doing that day.

Families now rarely gather at the evening dinner table. Many today do not even know what an evening dinner table is.

Fathers, mothers and children each have separate schedules, come and go, and barely make contact at any time during the day, except by cell phone. I recently met a family that in the evening ate from pickup food on plates from the island in the kitchen, individually, as each happened to pass that way.

This "new normal" makes implementing Deuteronomy 6:7 extremely challenging: *"You shall teach them diligently to your children, and shall talk of them when you sit in your house, and when you walk by the way, and when you lie down, and when you rise."* It makes leaving a godly legacy difficult, particularly for those of us in the 4th quarter. But, there are ways.

You must be the storyteller that is weaving the fabric of God's legacy about your life. Your children, grandchildren, nephews, and nieces desperately need to hear about your story so that they can pass it on to their children, so that each generation can know about the God who is faithful and worthy of trust; so that each generation may find their faith in Jesus Christ. Don't leave it to someone at your funeral to briefly and imperfectly tell your God-story. It's too important!

Here's what you can do. Along with telling your story at family dinners or other events, write it out in a journal, diary or book. The story can be told in an audio or video recording. Jean spent about two hours in front of the camera retelling the story of her life, including the story of her father and mother. In two hours, God's story reached back two generations—almost 200 years. It was all captured on a digital recording, now computer readable, for future generations to see and hear what wonderful things God did through her life and the life of her father and mother—how Christ transformed her life. Her dash didn't have to wait to be on a headstone.

I have heard and read many biographies. These are stories usually citing significant achievements. But too often they end with an empty bucket. Having done many important things, these stories come to an end, devoid of God's story in their lives. These stories will never be told in heaven. But, your story is different. It will last forever because it's God's story and reflects the presence of Christ in your life throughout the years.

Remember, you are either building a legacy to leave to your family or simply providing a dash between two dates on a headstone with no eternal significance. If your dash is only a story without Christ, the dash will remain undefined and eventually unknown and forgotten. It will be a story left untold with no eternal memorial stones.

What kind of legacy are you and I leaving for the generations to come? Will it be something that will strengthen their faith in God, provide encouragement, and be a source of blessings? Or will it be a blank page? Will it be a faith builder, or will it remain just a tiny mark on a headstone? A life without stones does not bring glory to God. *Speak it out! Write it out!* Make it a coherent, interesting story about your spiritual journey, about how Christ redeemed you and the things He did through you and for you. As you tell your story, *remember, God is never boring.*

Essential to your legacy story is your children's own legacy story. They need to have a personal relationship with Christ to carry forward into their children's lives, and so on. Remember, your legacy—your memorial stones—*alone* will never carry your children across the final goal line to hear, *"Well done good and faithful servant."* They must have their own personal encounter with Christ, and so must their children, and those after them. Each generation must have its own legacy—its own memorial stones—to pass on along with yours. Each generation discovers for themselves, with the help of your legacy story, forgiveness of sin and a new life in Christ to share with the next generation. That's what makes a godly legacy so powerful!

Such a legacy is the true treasure of life that keeps on giving and bearing dividends generation after generation. It is not an inheritance, but rather **a** wonderful enduring heritage! *This is a godly legacy!*

> *When is the best time to plant a tree? Twenty years ago!*
> *When is the second best time to plant a tree? Today!*
> *A Chinese Proverb*

Start today to craft a God story about His love for you, about how He faithfully led you throughout the journey of your life, and how He transformed your life through Jesus Christ. Then share it with your family. And make sure they share it with their families. It is really very simple, but it is extremely important to do. It's the *final score* on life's scoreboard. *It is never too late to begin leaving a godly legacy.*

Let's Talk About It

1. What is the greatest gift you can leave your family? What are you doing *now* in preparing your legacy gift?

2. What kind of stones, or memorials, are you leaving your family? Specifically, how are you doing that? In what ways will they remember your life-walk with the Lord?

3. Have you ever told your family the story of how God became important to you? How can you do that effectively considering the age span of your family, i.e., adult children, grand children, etc., and, perhaps over distances that separate them at this point in their lives?

4. Have you ever shared with them their need to have their own story about how the Lord has redeemed them, so they can pass their story along to their children and those they love?

Chapter 6

Wrap Up – What Is Your Life?

*O Lord, make me know my end and what is the measure
of my days; let me know how fleeting I am!
Behold, you have made my days a few handbreadths,
and my lifetime is as nothing before you.
Surely all mankind stands as a mere breath! Selah.
(Psalm 39:4–5)*

After the game is over, sport commentators and pundits review the game, recapturing the highlights of the plays and the players. With great enthusiasm, they point out what made the game special, and what you, as a viewer, should remember about the game. This is called the "wrap up."

God has his own wrap up at the end of our lives. Unlike the wrap up of the sport commentators and pundits, He has been telling us about the end from the beginning. He has been reminding us throughout the game about the brevity and temporal nature of our lives so that we can we can remain focused on what is truly important, make wise choices, and keep our eyes fixed on the goal. His point? Nothing will be said about us, after our life on earth is over, that He hasn't already told us. No wrap-up surprises. No "aha" moments.

God wants our attention. Sometimes to get our attention, He pulls us out of the game for a while, just as the coach may do in football. He is, after all, our Coach, our Owner! The circumstances may vary. Maybe it's the way we are playing. Maybe He senses we have lost our focus. In any case, we have all been there—maybe more than once. It could be a sudden illness, losing our job, or something major in our family. Whatever it is, our lives are interrupted. He makes us stop doing whatever it is we are doing and says, *"Be still and know that I am God."* This is when He pointedly reminds us, *"Remember who's in charge?"*

In the 4th quarter, we are forced to ponder, *"What is my life?"* If we pay attention to events that touch our lives in ways that call us "to be still," we know that it's God's time for us to reflect on what is truly important in life. He may pull us out of the game for a while so that we can think about what really matters in life.

Sometimes, we may be called to suffer for a season. God's glory is not laid aside in suffering. I deal with this subject in my book, *Learning to Suffer God's Way: Discovering Purpose in Suffering* (2012; Available at www.amazon.com). Our suffering—and there is a lot of it to go around—may be an opportunity for God to bless us, and the lives of those who are touched by our suffering. Our suffering may be God's way of asking us where Jesus Christ is in relationship to our life—do we just believe in Him or do we *know* Him, intimately. It is God's time for us to be still. It is time for us to reflect on, *"What is my life?"*

As we come to this haunting question, we may pull out our list of accomplishments. Well, let's see. I have my success stories, the plaques that hang on my wall, my wonderful life experiences at work, my family, and my church. Then, God's still small voice penetrates our overly saturated lives, *"That's really not the answer I was looking for! Let's try again. What is your life?"*

God's assessment of your life is simple:

> *For you are a mist (vapor) that appears for a little time and then vanishes. (James 4:14)*

If Jesus is not part of your story, then no matter what you have accomplished in life, no matter what wonderful things people can say about you, your life remains a mist that soon disappears—it's gone! How important it is to have Jesus Christ as your story, your legacy, in the 4th quarter! We want to be God's story throughout eternity. As a Friend, as a Coach, and as an Owner Jesus wants to tell His story through your life. As Savior, Lord, and Sovereign God He is ready whenever you are. He is the only way to live life to its fullest in the 4th quarter, with the knowledge that you are, in fact, *already* a winner in His eyes.

God's wrap-up question to you and to me is: *"What is your life?"* It's a question He has been asking throughout the game. It is the same question He will ask at the end of the game. It is the question He asks today. Is your dash only a mist that will vanish, or does it contain an eternal story that will be told, and retold throughout the ages because it is His story in you.

> *"For God so loved the world, that he gave his only Son, that whoever believes in him should not perish but have eternal life. (John 3:16)*

> *I give them eternal life, and they will never perish, and no one will snatch them out of my hand.*
> *(John 10:28)*

"What is your life?"

I write these things to you who believe in the name of the Son of God, that you may know that you have eternal life. (I John 5:13)

Let's Talk About It

1. As you approach the end of the 4th quarter, what brief words would you like see written on your headstone that would sum up your life? How do you want people to remember you?

2. In what ways has God stopped what you were doing for you to reflect and ask, "What is my life?" What are the things that define your life?

3. If you knew you when the "game" would be over (the 4th quarter) what would you do differently today?

4. The 4th quarter is about preparation: preparing now for then, getting ready in time to prepared for eternity. Describe how you are preparing today for eternity?

5. Based on John 3:16; John 10:28; and I John 5:13 what is the assurance we can have about our future beyond the grave?

One last thing. As part of the wrap up, write down three things you must do to get ready for the end of the 4th quarter. How will you carry them out, and when will you do them?

Your Notes:

Appendix

A 4th Quarter Poem

Only One Life . . .

Two little lines I heard one day,
Traveling along life's busy way;
Bringing conviction to my heart,
And from my mind would not depart;
Only one life, twill soon be past,
Only what's done for Christ will last.

Only one life, yes only one,
Soon will its fleeting hours be done;
Then, in 'that day' my Lord to meet,
And stand before His Judgment seat;
Only one life, 'twill soon be past,
Only what's done for Christ will last.

Only one life, a few brief years,
Each with its burdens, hopes, and fears;
Each with its days I must fulfill,
Living for self or in His will;
Only one life, 'twill soon be past,
Only what's done for Christ will last.

Give me Father, a purpose deep,
In joy or sorrow Thy word to keep;
Faithful and true what e'er the strife,
Pleasing Thee in my daily life;
 Only one life, 'twill soon be past,
Only what's done for Christ will last.

Now let me say,"Thy will be done";
And when at last I'll hear the call,
I know I'll say "twas worth it all";
Only one life,'twill soon be past,
Only what's done for Christ will last."

C.T. Studd (1860 – 1931)
English Missionary to China, India, and Africa

Made in the USA
Columbia, SC
11 July 2019